# DEALING WITH TOXIC RELATIONSHIP:

# A GUIDE ON HOW TO HEAL FROM TOXIC RELATIONSHIP

**Williams, C. Bower,**

# Table of Contents

## Chapter One
## Meaning of toxic relationship

A toxic relationship is one that causes you to feel unsupported, misconstrued, disparaged, or gone after. On a fundamental level, any relationship that exacerbates you as opposed to all the more likely can become toxic over the long run.

Toxic connections can exist in pretty much any specific circumstance, from the jungle gym to the meeting room to the bedroom. You might try to manage toxic connections among your relatives.

A relationship is toxic when your prosperity is compromised. Individuals with psychological maladjustments, like bipolar problems, significant discouragement, or even burdensome propensities, might be especially defenseless to toxic connections since they are as of now delicate to pessimistic feelings. Be that as it may, toxic individuals can influence anyone.

By definition, a toxic relationship is a relationship described by ways of behaving with respect to the harmful partner that are sincerely and, not inconsistently, genuinely harmful.

While a sound relationship adds to our confidence and close to home energy, a toxic relationship harms confidence and channels energy.

A solid relationship includes common consideration, regard, and sympathy; an interest in our partner's government assistance and development; and a capacity to share control and navigation.

To put it plainly, a solid relationship includes a common longing for one another's satisfaction. A sound relationship is a protected relationship, a relationship where we can act naturally and unafraid, where we feel great and secure.

A toxic relationship, then again, is definitely not a protected spot. A toxic relationship is defined by uncertainty, narcissism, predominance, and control. We risk our very being by remaining in such a relationship. To say a toxic relationship is useless is, best case scenario, a misrepresentation of the truth.

In a solid relationship, everything only sort of works. You could differ every once in a while or happen upon different obstacles, but you, for the most part, settle on choices together, straightforwardly examining any issues that emerge, and really appreciate each other's conversation.

Toxic connections are another story. In a toxic relationship, you could reliably feel depleted or despondent in the wake of investing energy in your partner.

Perhaps the relationship no longer feels at all agreeable, but you actually love your partner. For reasons unknown, you generally appear to annoy one another or apparently can't quit squabbling about minor issues. You could try and fear the possibility of seeing them, rather than anticipating it as you did previously.

## What is an Abusive Relationship?

An abusive relationship is any relationship that portrays dominance and control over a person in a relationship. The abuse can be emotional, physical, psychological, or sexual. The victim in an abusive relationship is often frightened, humiliated, hurt or terrorized, and is most afraid of moving out of the relationship. This type of relationship can happen to any person, regardless of gender, race, religion, or age. Also, people of different socio-economic statuses experience such relationships.

It is difficult to know if a person is abusive or not at the beginning of a relationship. However, after a period of interacting with such a person, there are warning signs that can make one avoid abusive individuals. Abusive relationships occur when the partners have settled, and there are fewer chances of them leaving each other. The abusive partner takes advantage, and turns the relationship into an abusive one. An abusive relationship maintains the struggles of one partner under the humiliation of another.

Forms and examples of an abusive relationship include physical abuse, sexual abuse, emotional abuse, and material abuse, to mention a few. In a statistic concerning victims of abuse, it was established that abused women are relatively many compared to men.

**Causes of Abusive Relationships**

There are various causes of abusive behavior in relationships. Some of them include:

- The need for the dominant partner to control the other
- The feeling of superiority in a relationship

- Lack of repercussions after abuse
- General insecurities that cause a person to suspect their partner of wrongdoing.

## The Effects of Abusive Relationships

Oppressive connections are improper in light of the fact that they do critical harm to the people in question. Casualties endure genuinely, mentally, and even financially. These impacts are talked about underneath:

## Physical Effects

Physical Abuse in Relationships: Victims of abusive relationships suffer from permanent injuries and scars resulting from physical abuse. A victim might have broken a limb during a fight or have been given a severe cut. The abuser does not reach this extent at once, but gradually develops the habit of physically abusing their partner. After several light physical cases of abuse, the abuser goes extreme and tries to kill their partner. In such a situation, a victim is left with a physical scar or permanent damage to a part of their body.

There are other long-term effects, like high blood pressure and heart disease, that may arise from abusive relationships. Victims develop such ailments after a long time of torture and abuse. If they are not assisted immediately, a victim can succumb to the effects of abuse.

**Psychological Effects**

Many psychological effects arise from abusive relationships. The most common are PTSD (Post-traumatic stress disorder) causing depression and anxiety, and the general mental health of a person. Individuals who suffer from these conditions have a difficult time relating to other people. They might not even engage in other relationships due to the negative experience they have in them.

Psychological effects can have advanced issues on individuals since they can limit their ability to attend school if they are students, or avoid going to work.

They might also try to seek refuge from drugs and develop other significant problems like addiction. Consequently, conditions like malnutrition can arise when a person overeats or undereats. If the person undereats, there are diseases that are likely to affect them, and the same is true with overeating. Therefore, psychological effects can be diverse and could lead to many more problems for the victims.

**The distinction between abuse and toxicity**

Toxicity in a relationship can take many forms, including emotional or verbal abuse. Still, it's not always possible to draw a clear line between toxicity and abuse.

Toxic relationships are unhealthy, but they're not necessarily abusive. Sometimes, toxic behavior isn't intentional — though, of course, that doesn't make it any less hurtful. Keep in mind, too, that many unhealthy relationships involve toxic behavior from both partners, even when neither partner behaves in an abusive way.

Abuse, on the other hand, stems from a desire to hold power over someone else and control their behavior. Since abuse often happens gradually and in subtle ways, you may not always recognize it easily, especially if the relationship has been toxic for some time.

There's never an excuse for abusive behavior. Though change is possible for anyone, you can't make your partner change. They have to choose that route themselves.

Chronic stress, anxiety, or doubt

It's typical to have periods of frustration with your partner or doubts about your future together. But you shouldn't spend significant amounts of time worrying about the relationship or your safety.

An abusive partner might say things that make you doubt the security of the relationship, or even your own self-worth:

"You're lucky." I'm with you. I could have anyone. "

**Separation from friends and family**

Sometimes, dealing with a toxic relationship can lead you to withdraw from friends and family. But an abusive partner may forcefully distance you from your support network.

They might snatch your phone while you're talking, answer it for you and say you're busy, or make such a fuss when you say you have plans that you end up canceling. They may also convince you that your loved ones don't want to hear from you, anyway.

**Interference with work or school**

An abusive partner may prevent you from seeking employment or studying in order to isolate and control you.

They may also attempt to humiliate you at your workplace or school by causing a scene, talking to your boss or teachers, or lying to your co-workers and classmates.

## Fear and intimidation

An abusive partner might explode with rage or use intimidation tactics, such as slamming their fists into walls or not allowing you to leave the house during a fight.

## Name-calling and put-downs

A boisterous attack is intended to humiliate and belittle your preferences, appearance, or accomplishments.

## Financial restrictions

A few methods of financial abuse are:

They try to manage the money that comes in by preventing you from knowing your financial standing; restricting your access to credit cards; providing you with a daily remittance; and encouraging you to ask for more.

**Gas lighting**

Gas lighting is a control technique that causes you to doubt your emotions, impulses, and mental stability.

When someone is trying to gaslight you, they might: demand that something you remember never happened; admit they never said something when you remember them saying it; or accuse you of having anger and control issues.

**Threats of self-harm**

A control tactic is to take actions that could hurt themselves to pressure you into taking action.

If they start to self-destruct, take them seriously and advise them to contact a hotline for immediate assistance. Simply realize that supporting them doesn't mean consenting to what they need.

**Physical violence**

Dangers and verbal put-downs can heighten actual viciousness. If your partner is pushing, pushing, or hitting you, it's a clear sign that the relationship has become dangerous.

**Chapter Two**
**How to identify toxic relationships**

At the point when you're in a toxic relationship, you may not necessarily find it simple to see the warnings springing up. It's no different either; you could see a portion of these signs in yourself, your partner, or the actual relationship.

**Lack of support**

"Healthy relationships are based on a mutual desire to see the other succeed in all areas of life," But when things turn toxic, every achievement becomes a competition.

In short, the time you spend together no longer feels positive. You don't feel supported or encouraged, and you can't trust them to show up for you. Instead, you might get the impression that your needs and interests don't matter, that they only care about what they want.

**Toxic communication**

Rather than thoughtfulness and common regard, the vast majority of your discussions are loaded up with mockery or analysis and energized by disdain.

Do you discover yourself offering inconsiderate comments to your companions or relatives? Perhaps you rehash what they said in a ridiculing tone when they're in another room. You might try and begin evading their calls, just to get a break from the inescapable contention and antagonism.

**Envy or jealousy**

While it's completely fine to encounter a little jealousy occasionally, it can turn into an issue on the off chance that your jealousy holds you back from contemplating your partner's victories.

The equivalent goes for desire. Indeed, it's a completely normal human inclination. Be that as it may, when it prompts consistent doubt and questions, it can rapidly start to disintegrate your relationship.

## Controlling behaviors

Does your partner constantly ask where you are? Perhaps they become irritated or aggravated when you don't promptly answer texts or text you severally until you do.

These ways of behaving could come from desire or the absence of trust. However, they can likewise suggest a requirement for control—the two of which can add to the relationship's toxicity.

## Resentment

Holding on to grudges and letting them fester chips away at intimacy.

Over time, frustration or resentment can build up and make a smaller chasm much bigger.

Note, too, whether you tend to nurse these grievances quietly because you don't feel safe speaking up when something bothers you. Your relationship could be toxic if you can't trust your partner to listen to your concerns.

**Dishonesty**

You wind up continually making up lies about your whereabouts or whom you get together with—whether that is because you need to try not to invest energy in your partner or because you stress how they'll respond assuming you come clean with them.

**Patterns of disrespect**

Being chronically late, casually "forgetting" events, and other behaviors that show disrespect for your time are a red flag.

Keep in mind that some people may truly struggle with making and keeping plans on time, so it may help to start with a conversation about this behavior. If it's not intentional, you might notice some improvement after you explain why it bothers you.

## Negative financial behavior

Sharing finances with a partner often involves some level of agreement about how you'll spend or save your money. That said, it's not necessarily toxic if one partner chooses to spend money on items the other partner doesn't approve of.

It can be toxic, though, if you've come to an agreement about your finances and one partner constantly disrespects that agreement.

## Constant stress

Conventional life challenges, such as a relative's illness or a job loss, can put a strain on your relationship. In any case, being constantly nervous, even when you're not under pressure from outside sources, is a red flag that something is wrong.

This constant pressure can harm your physical and psychological well-being, and you may feel hopeless, intellectually and physically depleted, or, in general, unwell.

## Ignoring your needs

Obliging anything that your partner needs to do, in any event when it conflicts with your desires or comfort level, is a certain indication of toxicity.

**Lost relationships**

You've quit investing energy in loved ones, either to stay away from the struggle with your partner or to get around making sense of what's going on in your relationship.

On the other hand, you could track down that managing your partner (or agonizing over your relationship) possesses quite a bit of your leisure time.

**Lack of self-care**

In a toxic relationship, you could relinquish your standard of self-care propensities.

You could pull out of leisure activities you once cherished, disregard your wellbeing, and penance your available energy. This could happen because you don't have the energy for these exercises or because your partner dislikes it when you do whatever you might feel like doing.

## Expecting change

You could remain in the relationship since you recollect the amount of fun you had in the first place. Perhaps you imagine that, on the off chance that you simply change yourself and your activities, they'll change also.

## Treading lightly

You stress that by raising issues, you'll incite outrageous pressure, so you become a struggle avoidant and remain quiet about any issues.

## Decreased self-esteem

Your partner faults you for all that turns out badly and causes you to feel as though you can do nothing right. They might do this by disparaging, excusing, or humiliating you in broad daylight.

**Chapter Three**

**How to deal with toxic partners in a relationship.**

Many individuals accept that toxic relationships are ill-fated, but that isn't generally the situation.

The game changer? The two partners should need to change. If, by some stroke of good luck, one partner puts resources into making sound examples, there is tragically little probability that change will happen.

A couple of signs you could figure out things together:

• Acknowledgment of obligation

On the off chance that both you and your partner realize the relationship is battling and need to further develop it, you're in good shape.

Perceiving past ways of behaving that have hurt the relationship is indispensable for the two to finish. It mirrors an interest in mindfulness and self-obligation.

To put it another way, the two partners ought to acknowledge their part in adding to the toxicity, from disdain to desire to not taking a stand in opposition to worries and disillusionments.

- Eagerness to contribute

Are you and your partner ready to put resources into improving the relationship? That is a decent sign.

This might appear as an interest in developing discussions or saving customary blocks of time for getting to know each other.

- Shift from blaming to understanding

On the off chance that you're both ready to control the discussion away from accusing and more toward understanding and realizing, there might be a way ahead.

- Receptiveness to outside help

Some of the time, you could require help to get things in the groove again, either through individual or couple directing.

There's no shame in getting proficient assistance to address predictable relationship issues. Some of the time, you can't get on with everything, adding to the toxicity from inside the relationship, and relationship instructors are prepared to offer a nonpartisan point of view and unprejudiced help.

They can likewise show you new methodologies for tending to and settling struggles, making it To make better examples that stick.

**Step-by-step instructions to manage the toxic relationship and keep your mental stability**

These tools can assist you with making something happen.

**Try not to choose not to move on.**

Without a doubt, part of fixing the relationship will probably include tending to previous occasions. Be that as it may, this ought not to be the sole focal point of your relationship.

Oppose the compulsion to continually allude back to negative situations, since this can leave both of you tense, disappointed, and fundamentally right back where you began.

**View your band together with sympathy.**

At the point when you wind up needing to blame your partner for every one of the issues in the house, have a go at making a stride back and checking It reveals the expected inspirations behind their way of behaving.

Have they as of late gone through a difficult time at work? Had some family show weighed vigorously at the forefront of their thoughts?

These difficulties don't pardon a terrible way of behaving; however, they can assist you with coming to a superior understanding of where it comes from.

**Begin treatment**

A receptiveness to treatment can be a decent sign that retouching the relationship is conceivable. To help the relationship, push ahead. However, you'll have to come up with a plan for that first arrangement.

While couple directing is a decent beginning stage, individual treatment can be a useful tool.

expansion. Individual treatment offers a place of refuge to investigate connection issues and different variables that could add to relationship concerns. It additionally assists you with getting a better understanding of toxic ways of behaving versus oppressive ones.

**Practice solid correspondence.**

Give close consideration to how you converse with one another as you retouch things. Be delicate with one another and attempt to stay away from mockery and, surprisingly, gentle punches.

Additionally, it centers around utilizing "I" articulations, particularly while discussing relationship issues.

For instance, rather than saying, "You don't pay attention to what I'm talking about," you could say, "I feel hurt when you take out your telephone while I'm talking since it gives me the feeling that what I say doesn't make any difference."

**Be responsible**

The two partners should recognize their part in cultivating the toxic relationship.

This implies distinguishing and assuming a sense of ownership of your own decisions in the relationship. It additionally implies focusing on remaining present and connected during troublesome discussions, rather than keeping away from those conversations or intellectually looking at them.

**Recuperate independently.**

Every one of you genuinely should independently figure out what you want from the relationship and where your limits lie,

Regardless of whether you feel like you know your requirements and limits, it merits returning to them and afterwards imparting them to your partner.

Talking through limits is a decent initial step. Keep in mind, however, that limits are adaptable, so it's essential to continue to talk about them as they change over the long run.

The method involved in reconstructing a harmed relationship offers a decent chance to reconsider how you feel about specific components of the relationship, from correspondence requirements to actual closeness.

**Hold space for each other's change.**

Keep in mind  that things won't change for the time being. Throughout the next few months, cooperate on being adaptable and patient with one another as you develop.

**Chapter Four**

**Steps to Heal from Different Types of Toxicity**

**How to Take Care of Yourself After Your Toxic Relationship Ends**

**1. Try not to allow that individual to reside in your heart**

Our loved ones will generally possess a spot in our souls, and a piece of that goes with them when they leave. Be that as it may, you don't need to maintain this viewpoint! You will without a doubt feel unfulfilled. However, allow yourself to recuperate. You don't need to despise that individual - just let them go for the last time.

**2. Show restraint toward Yourself**

Recuperating from a toxic relationship won't find lasting success on the off chance that you are not patient with yourself. Allow yourself to recuperate, regardless of how long it takes.

It is understood that if you are separated from somebody and restarting your existence without them takes time. You might fly off the handle, restless, and disappointed while recuperating. Be that as it may, attempt to remain mentally collected and be thoughtful and delicate with yourself.

On the off chance that you wouldn't agree with another person, then, at that point, don't express it to yourself. All things being equal, compose positive considerations and read them in the wake of strolling up and before hitting the sack.

## 3. Embrace Who You Are

Terrible connections can cause you to genuinely regret them. You might think it is just your shortcoming and what you have done isn't correct. Be that as it may, you want to think the alternate way round! Remain firm any place you are - audacious and unstoppable.

Rehearsing self-acknowledgement can further develop your close-to-home prosperity. In any case, that doesn't mean you don't need to acknowledge your negatives. Embrace your excellencies. Additionally, you should acknowledge your negative characteristics and attempt to chip away at them.

## 4. Try not to Think You Are a Victim

Dispose of your casualty attitude, as it will take away your power and autonomy. All things being equal, view yourself as a comeback to life like a phoenix and be prepared to conquer obstructions.

## 5. Gain New Experiences

Relinquish the past and plan to carry on with your life in another manner. Gain new experiences and do new things that interest you the most. Take on testing undertakings and enjoy leisure activities with those who love you.

On the off chance that you love traveling, plan an end-of-the-week escape with your mates. Take photos on the way, attempt new food varieties, meet new individuals, and partake for the sake of entertainment exercises. When you are back from the excursion, remember those minutes, and plan your next trip.

## 6. Conquer Negative Thoughts

Try not to permit negative contemplations to lease a space to you. One method for disposing of them is by rehearsing contemplation. Begin and end your day with a brilliant grin all over. Practice thankfulness and get some downtime from your timetable to chip in for a social reason.

## 7. Figure What You Want From A Relationship

You can begin by contemplating what you need from your relationship before plunging into possibilities. Distinguish your qualities and search for them in your next significant other.

Do you want somebody who can assist you with satisfying your expert objectives? Or on the other hand, an individual who can impart successfully? Understand that you merit a sound relationship and the sort of affection and care you will provide for other people. Try not to hurry into a relationship based on the premise that you want somebody. Take as much time as

You need to recuperate and find the sort of individual you need in your life.

Toxic connections can adversely influence your psychological well-being and are difficult to manage. They additionally influence your confidence and appear to be threatening. Be that as it may, how do you recuperate from a toxic relationship? Observing the no-contact guideline, pardoning yourself, and zeroing in on the present might help recuperate from a toxic relationship.

Consequently, leave all the antagonism and distinguish the fundamental issues that cause toxicity in the relationship. Focus on your psychological prosperity and converse with your specialist concerning your emotional well-being. Furthermore, defining limits, rehearsing, taking care of oneself, and encircling yourself with

Positivity might help dispose of toxic individuals.

Leaving a toxic relationship is a courageous step that everybody deserves the opportunity to take. In any case, separating accompanies pressure, nervousness, and feelings that should be handled. That is valid even after a sound relationship. Returning quickly takes time. However, there are ways of supporting your excursion all through.

Ways to recuperate from a toxic relationship aren't very similar for everybody. It's an interaction unique to your encounters and circumstances. All things considered, toxic partners frequently share a couple of ways of behaving. Understanding what they are can assist us with understanding how to recuperate from them.

## What's the most effective way to heal when you're in a new, sound relationship?

Framing new bonds after a toxic relationship is difficult, but doing it continuously is worth celebrating as well. A sign you've made considerable progress, and the right partner can improve things significantly.

**Eagerness to help**

You're recuperating is the characteristic of a decent partner. All things considered, getting into a sound and secure relationship doesn't mean the recuperating system is finished.

The toxicity of a past relationship can follow you into another one, particularly the principal relationship after separation.

At the point when we're continually encircled by pressure, strain, and nervousness, we foster adapting propensities. While these propensities assist us with controlling our sentiments when we're overwhelmed, they're well defined for toxic conditions.

Conduct created in a toxic relationship is seldom adaptable to a healthy one. First of all, your partner is unique.

Somebody who speaks with compassion, approves of your interests, and takes responsibility for making an open space for both of you to flourish. They might raise concerns all the more promptly, accepting for the time being that they're the only things to deal with. You might have figured out how to contend forcefully with a toxic partner  or have the propensity for stalling.

## Center around the present

Zeroing in on the current means understanding that your adapting propensities weren't shaped by your ongoing relationship. Care activities can assist with establishing our considerations in the now, not the past.

By doing this, you give yourself the clarity to respond to your ongoing reality. It creates a limit between the toxic relationship and the association you're attempting to work with your new partner.

## Fabricate an emotionally supportive network.

A steady partner is amazing. However, they can rarely give us all the help we want. Regardless of whether they're willing and able to attempt it, they will not have every one of the instruments to help.

Oppressive individuals will frequently remove their partner from companions, family, councilors—anybody who can move power back to the weak partner. Reconstructing that encouraging group of people is a fundamental piece of recuperating.

**Impart what you want to do with your partner.**

Your new partner might do or offer something that worries you, regardless of whether they have only well-meaning goals. You're finding out about one another right off the bat in a relationship. It is indispensable to communicate your requirements and sentiments.

Indeed, a caring partner can explore what they're mindful of. It's all right on the off chance that you're not happy delving into every one of the subtleties or talking about an ex by any stretch of the imagination.

The key here is to advise your partner enough to clarify their choices and ways to deal with the relationship.


**How to Heal when you've just left a toxic relationship**

Saying a final farewell to a toxic partner is a courageous step. More than that, it's the initial step to reconstructing your life. You can't recuperate while effectively being harmed, particularly around individuals who control and discredit your sentiments.

The difficulty comes when we treat separation as the last step and not the first. A great deal of the time, this stage is the point at which the genuine gravity of what you're feeling sinks in. The weeks following a separation can be misunderstood for that definite explanation.

A toxic relationship simply tosses a lot at you. Being overpowered, in shock, and battling to deal with encounters are indications of injury. We can begin attempting to deal with the toxicity once we emerge from endurance mode. Its sheer power can be jarring. However, this is the very thing that you can do:

**Permit yourself to feel**

When somebody is committed to discrediting you, understanding your feelings can be hard. Uncertainty, disarray, and even responsibility can kick in. Denying and keeping away from your sentiments is how they develop. You want to allow yourself to sit with them.

**Try not to contact your ex-partner**

However, as depleting as a poisonous relationship seems to be, getting out of it very well may startle you from the get-go. You're not leaving a safe place—toxicity isn't encouraging—but you are in a profoundly new area.

Out of nowhere, you have autonomy and additional obligations. With that comes the requirement for abilities and backing that might have been disregarded not long ago. The compulsion to withdraw can be perfect. However, don't contact your ex.

Part of sitting with horrendous encounters is perceiving how weak they make us. A poisonous partner will control that weakness to recapture control over you. The best thing for your recuperation is to never allow them the opportunity.

**Rediscover yourself as a person.**

Freedom can be scary. However, recollect that it's great. Everyone has the right to have their independence, nobility, and singularity safeguarded.

Becoming familiar with your autonomy is great for your recuperating venture. This is an ideal opportunity to zero in on what you need and need in your life. This is the point at which your objectives, dreams, and viewpoints become a need once more.

## How to Heal when you and your new partner both had past toxic relationships

Much like you, your new partner will come into the relationship with their own set of experiences. On the off chance that you've both experienced toxic relationships in the past, it implies you're both recuperating somehow or another.

While this can assist you with understanding one another, it should be done strongly. The idea of injury holding has been weakened by open talk. It isn't the point at which you interface with somebody over a shared injury. All things being equal, it's the personal conduct standard an oppressive partner uses to keep control while harming you.

**Understanding and showing restraint toward one another can help you both recuperate.**

An injury bond maneuvers an individual toward enduring and in any event, legitimizing misuse. A disregarded individual can cut off this bond despite everything and leave with a distorted comprehension of what loyalty and closeness ought to resemble. That is the reason it's so essential to recuperate beyond a relationship first, or if nothing else at the same time.

**Make space to share encounters**

It begins with having sufficient room to be open to one another. However, space isn't simply making time to discuss things. It's tied in with having solid limits between the connections so toxicity can't crawl into the enhanced one.

**Show restraint toward one another.**

It isn't difficult to talk about things. Indeed, even in day-to-day existence, you will not necessarily know the proper behavior or how to respond to one another. You may not realize an activity causes grinding until it does. That goes for your partner as well.

At the point when individuals in a relationship are focused on persistence, botches don't become lethal. Partners support each other in observing better approaches to collaborate. Toward the day's end, that takes care of additional issues than you can envision for the long haul.

**Practice thoughtfulness**

While rehearsing persistence, remember to rehearse thoughtfulness as well. You're permitted to be disappointed with your partner as well.

The other way around, how you treat each other in those minutes  matters more than the actual issue, given it's resolvable.

Thoughtfulness is proactive. It fabricates the climate you need to live in long after you've quit responding to past toxicity. It makes a way for you both, one that prompts a better bond over the long haul.

www.ingramcontent.com/pod-product-compliance
Lightning Source LLC
Chambersburg PA
CBHW061722130726
47996CB00006B/2444